TRUE-LIFE PIRATES

Captain Kidd

Cavendish
Square

New York

Rebecca Stefoff

Published in 2015 by Cavendish Square Publishing, LLC
243 5th Avenue, Suite 136, New York, NY 10016

Library of Congress Cataloging-in-Publication Data

Stefoff, Rebecca, 1951-
Captain Kidd / Rebecca Stefoff.
pages cm. — (True-life pirates)
Includes bibliographical references and index.
ISBN 978-1-50260-205-3 (hardcover) ISBN 978-1-50260-204-6 (ebook)
1. Kidd, William, -1701—Juvenile literature. 2. Pirates—Great Britain—Biography—Juvenile literature. 3. Pirates—Indian Ocean—History—17th century—Juvenile literature. I. Title.

G537.K5S74 2015
910.4'5—dc23
[B]

2014015957

Editor: Andrew Coddington
Copy Editor: Cynthia Roby
Art Director: Jeffrey Talbot
Designer: Amy Greenan

Senior Production Manager: Jennifer Ryder-Talbot
Production Editor: David McNamara
Photo Research: J8 Media

The photographs in this book are used by permission and through the courtesy of: Cover photo, Hulton Archive/Getty Images, Greg Johnston/ Lonely Planet Images/Getty Images; Hulton Archive/Getty Images, 1, 14; Howard Pyle/File:Pyle pirates burying2.jpg/Wikimedia Commons, 4; Rigobert Bonne/File:1780 Bonne Map of Southern India, Ceylon, and the Maldives - Geographicus - IndiaSouth-bonne-1780.jpg/Wikimedia Commons, 7; B Cole/File:Blackbeard the Pirate - A General History of the Pyrates (1725), 70 - BL.jpg/Wikimedia Commons, 9; fdecomite/ File:Pirate Flag (6084517123).jpg/Wikimedia Commons, 11; Howard Pyle/File:Pyle pirate tales.jpg/Wikimedia Commons, 13; John Slezer/ File:Dundee1693 JohnSlezer2.jpg/Wikimedia Commons, 16; DEA PICTURE LIBRARY/De Agostini/Getty Images, 17; Johannes Vingboons/ File:GezichtOpNieuwAmsterdam.jpg/Wikimedia Commons, 19; Apic/Hulton Archive/Getty Images, 22; DEA/G. DAGLI ORTI/De Agostini/ Getty Images, 25; Peter Newark Pictures/The Bridgeman Art Library, 28; Print Collector/Hulton Archive/Getty Images, 32; © North Wind Picture Archives, 35; Courtesy Indiana University, 39.

Cover and interior design elements: (pirate map) Vera Petruk/Shutterstock.com; (rope on old paper) Irina Tischenko/Hemera/Thinkstock; (skull and crossbones) Tatiana Akhmetgalieva/Shutterstock.com; (crossed swords) Fun Way Illustration/Shutterstock.com; (old map elements) Man_Half-tube/iStock Vectors/Getty Images; (pirate flag) fdecomite/File:Pirate Flag (6084517123).jpg/Wikimedia Commons; (ship) Makhnach_S/ Shutterstock.com; (anchor) File:Anchor Pictogram.svg/Wikimedia Commons.

Printed in the United States of America

Contents

one

The Pirates of the Indian Ocean

Sick and weary from a year in prison, a man stood in a crowded courtroom to hear the charges against him. The year was 1701. The place was London, England. The prisoner was a middle-aged sea captain named William Kidd. He had been brought from Rhode Island, one of England's **colonies** in America, to stand trial.

When the charges against him were read aloud, Kidd received a horrible shock. He already knew that he would be charged with **piracy**. Now Kidd learned for the first time that he would also be tried for a second serious crime: murder. If he were found guilty of either crime, he faced the death penalty.

Captain Kidd Buries His Treasure, a painting by American artist Howard Pyle.

"William Kidd," the court clerk asked, "art thou guilty or not guilty?"

"Not guilty," said Captain William Kidd.

"How will you be tried?" the clerk asked.

Kidd answered, "By God and my country."

"God send you a good deliverance," the clerk said to Kidd.

Kidd begged the court for time to defend himself against the charge of piracy. Certain papers, Kidd claimed, would prove that he was innocent, if only he could get his hands on them.

Sir John Hawles, the chief lawyer for the **Crown**, agreed to send for a witness who might be able to help Kidd fight the piracy charge. However, in the very next moment, Hawles said that Kidd's murder trial would start right away.

That very afternoon, Captain William Kidd went on trial for the murder of William Moore, a sailor who had been one of his crewmen. Kidd must have hoped desperately for a stroke of luck that would save his life. Perhaps he felt that it was time for him to get lucky. He had not been much of a success as a pirate.

Was Kidd really a pirate? Even today, historians still argue about that question. Kidd's career at sea was mixed up with politics, war, greed, and betrayal. It took place in what has been called the **Golden Age of Piracy**.

The Golden Age of Piracy lasted from the 1680s to about 1730. During the first few years, pirates from Europe, England, and the American colonies swarmed in the waters of the Indian Ocean.

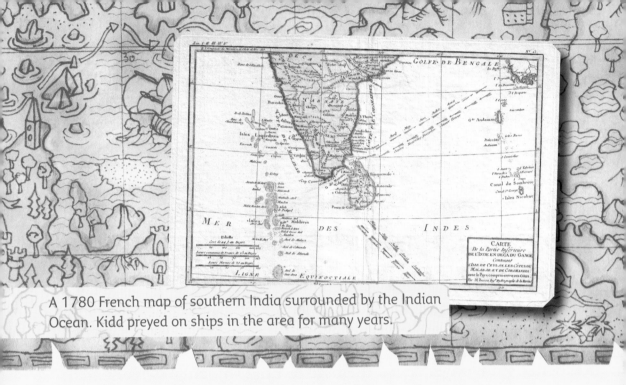

A 1780 French map of southern India surrounded by the Indian Ocean. Kidd preyed on ships in the area for many years.

The Riches of the Indian Ocean

The Indian Ocean is a large body of water located between Africa and Australia. It washes the shores of India, where England, France, Portugal, and the Netherlands set up **trading posts** during the Golden Age of Piracy. Beyond India are the islands of Indonesia, which were claimed at that time by the Netherlands.

The Indian Ocean had a long history of piracy. So did the Arabian Sea, the part of the Indian Ocean that lies between Arabia and India. For centuries Arab and Indian pirates had looted ships as they made their way through these waters, along the coasts of Africa, Arabia, and Persia (now called Iran). After European nations set up trading posts on the coasts of the Indian Ocean, a new crop of pirates from Europe and America joined in the action.

A Pirates' Paradise?

According to legend, so many European and American pirates hung out on Madagascar that a pirate society formed on the island. The name of this society was Libertatia, or Libertalia—either way, it meant "land of the free." The pirates who joined together to form Libertatia no longer called themselves Englishmen, or Frenchmen, or Americans, or Dutchmen. They called themselves **Liberi**.

The Liberi made their own laws, the most important being that all men were equal. There were no high-ranking nobles in the pirate group, and no slaves. The Liberi made all decisions by voting, and they chose their own leaders.

The Liberi also shared everything. Whenever one of their ships stopped another vessel on the high seas and looted it, the victorious pirates shared their **booty** with all of the other Liberi. They welcomed anyone who wanted to join them—and many crewmen from the trade ships switched sides and joined the pirate group, thinking that their lives would be better in a freedom-loving, independent pirate society. Captives who did not want to join were always set free.

Page 70

Blackbeard the Pirate.

This sketch from Johnson's book is of the pirate Blackbeard.

Do the Liberi sound too good to be true? Sadly, they probably never existed.

Pirates did spend time on Madagascar—there is no doubt of that. However, there is only one source of information about the pirates' paradise of Libertatia. That source is a book entitled *A General History of the Robberies & Murders of the Most Notorious Pyrates*. It was published in 1724, after most of the famous Madagascar pirates were dead.

Today, most experts agree that Captain Charles Johnson, author of the *General History*, invented the story of Libertatia. Why? Maybe he wanted to paint a picture of a society that sounded perfect, even if it was imaginary. Or perhaps he had heard garbled stories about the pirates on Madagascar, and wove them together to make his own book more interesting.

Trade ships from Europe carried cloth, manufactured goods, and gold and silver across the Indian Ocean to the trading posts. At the trading posts, the European goods and money were exchanged for valuable Asian goods such as silk, spices, tea, and fine Chinese pottery.

Two companies controlled most of this trade: the English East India Company, and the Dutch East India Company. Their ships were the richest **prizes** that pirates could hope to take. These rich **Indiamen**, as the company ships were called, were not always easy prey. Many were fast and heavily armed. Still, they often drew pirate attacks.

The raiders who prowled the Indian Ocean often stopped at Madagascar, a large island off the coast of Africa. There they could get supplies, especially fresh water and food. Madagascar had lots of good ports where ships could safely anchor, and the native people of the island were not hostile. By the 1690s, Madagascar had become the favorite haunt of many pirates.

Pirate or Privateer?

The stories of pirates' lives are often hard to sort out. That's because many pirates of the seventeenth and eighteenth centuries were pirates only part of the time. At other times they were respectable sea captains. Many priates also spent time as **privateers**.

A pirate unlawfully attacked a ship at sea in order to seize its cargo, the passengers and their valuables, or the ship itself. A privateer did many of the same things, with one important difference: unlike pirates,

Pirates used several kinds of flags to terrify other ships. This one was called the Jolly Roger, or skull-and-crossbones.

whose actions broke the law of every land, privateers were acting under the law of their own countries.

A privateer was supposed to attack *only* the ships of countries that were at war with his own nation. The legal permission to carry out these attacks was a document called a **letter of marque**. Letters of marque spelled out just what type of vessels a privateer was allowed to prey upon, and what was to be done with prisoners and loot.

The difference between a pirate and a privateer could be murky. Sometimes privateers joined actual sea battles between warring navies to attack ships of an enemy nation, just as their country's naval vessels would do. Most of the time, though, privateers acted more like pirates.

They disabled and looted enemy ships one at a time. The loot was doled out among the officers of the privateering ship, its crew, and the **investors**, who were the people who had helped pay for the ship and supplies in exchange for a share of the loot.

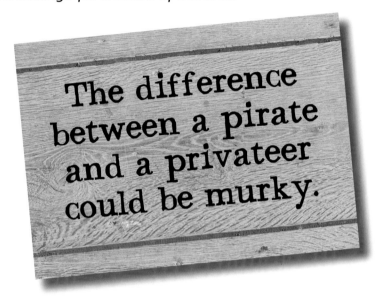

The difference between a pirate and a privateer could be murky.

The Trouble with Tew

A captain might set out as a privateer and then become a pirate. That's what happened to Thomas Tew, a respectable sea captain from a well-known Rhode Island family. In 1690, he moved to Bermuda, an island off the east coast of the United States in the North Atlantic Ocean. Like Rhode Island, Bermuda was an English colony, and Tew was an English citizen.

England was at war with France, so Tew became a privateer and was awarded permission to attack French ships. Before long, Tew had convinced his crew that they should turn to piracy. They headed for the Indian Ocean,

Pirate Thomas Tew (left) chats with New York Governor Benjamin Fletcher.

hoping to gain their fortunes by preying upon ships traveling the trade routes. After a stop in Madagascar, they headed north and captured an Arab merchant ship. That adventure made them all rich. Tew then returned to Rhode Island and took up the life of a gentleman.

Soon, however, Tew was eager to return to sea. In 1694, Benjamin Fletcher, the governor of the New York colony, gave Tew another letter of marque for privateering. Once again, Tew set out to sea as a privateer but turned to piracy instead.

By 1696, the English Crown saw Tew as a dangerous threat to shipping. King William III appointed a **pirate-hunter** to bring Tew down: Captain William Kidd.

two

Kidd's Early Life

The lives of pirates are full of unanswered questions. Many lived in an age when accurate records of births and deaths were not always kept. Sometimes pirates created mysteries by using false names. They did this to protect their families at home, or because they were only part-time pirates and wanted to live at ease in society when they weren't out pirating.

William Kidd did not use a false name. In spite of this fact, details about his early years remain scarce.

A popular image of bloodthirsty Captain Kidd from around 1700.

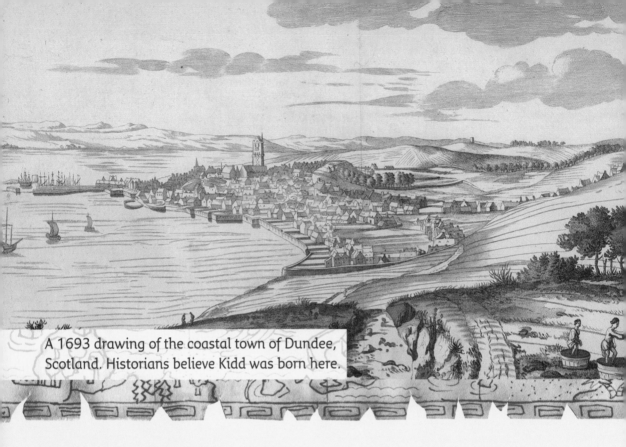

A 1693 drawing of the coastal town of Dundee, Scotland. Historians believe Kidd was born here.

A Son of Scotland

The date of Kidd's birth is not known for certain. Most sources say he was born in 1654 in Scotland, which lies just north of England. (England and Scotland would join together to become Great Britain in 1707.) He was most likely born in the port city of Dundee. There were rumors that Kidd's father was a sea captain, or at least a seafaring man.

As far as solid facts go, historians have not been able to learn when and where Kidd first went to sea. As a full-grown man, he was more than just a sailor—he had the skill and experience needed to captain a ship.

The *Blessed William*

The first information about Kidd comes from the late 1680s. At that time, England and France were at war. Privateers from each country attacked the other country's ships. Both nations had colonies on some of the islands that dot the Caribbean Sea, so this region was the scene of many attacks by privateers—and pirates.

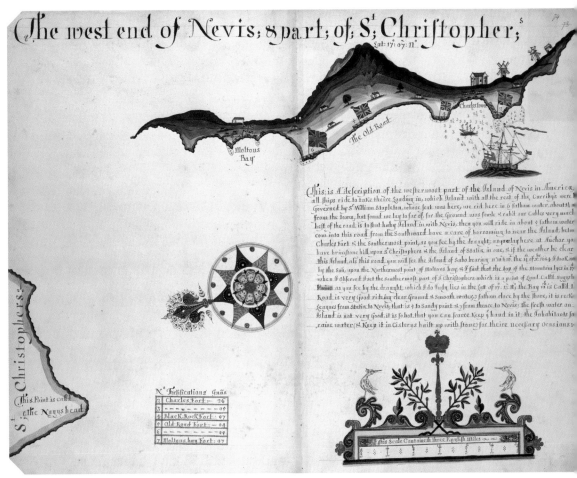

The Caribbean island of Nevis, where Kidd's privateering career began.

Which was Kidd? There are several versions of the story. In one version, Kidd was part of a pirate crew in the Caribbean in the 1680s. He and some other members of the crew took control of the pirate ship and sailed it to the English colony of Nevis, a small Caribbean island. The governor of the colony then granted them permission to serve as privateers instead of pirates.

Another version says that Kidd started out by serving on an English privateer vessel. When the privateers seized a French ship, Kidd was made captain of that ship. He renamed it the *Blessed William* in honor of the English king, and then went to Nevis to become a privateer on his own.

How Kidd got to Nevis may never be known for sure. Either way, he did show up there with the *Blessed William*, and the governor made Kidd an official privateer in 1689 or 1690.

Kidd and his ship became part of a fleet of privateers assigned to protect Nevis from the French. In return, the privateers could seize French ships and property. They attacked and looted the island of Marie-Galante, a French colony. Soon afterward, members of Kidd's crew decided to become pirates. While Kidd was away from the *Blessed William* on shore, they took off in the ship, leaving their captain behind.

One of the ringleaders of the group that deserted Kidd was named Robert Culliford. The two men's paths would cross again. Kidd would also face another betrayal by his crew. First, though, he would sail north, away from the Caribbean and toward a fresh start in life.

New York was becoming a busy harbor in the 1690s when Captain Kidd started a new life there.

A New Life in New York

After the loss of the *Blessed William*, the governor of Nevis gave Kidd another ship so that he could chase Culliford and the other crewmen who had stolen the *William*. The chase led to New York City, but Kidd did not capture the *William*. Instead he learned that Culliford and the others had joined a pirate crew bound for the Indian Ocean.

Kidd must have liked New York, because he decided to stay there. In 1691, he bought a house from a young woman named Sarah Bradley Cox Oort, who came from a well-known New York family. Oort was married to a wealthy man and had also inherited money from her first husband, who had died.

Kidd became Oort's third husband when they married in May 1691. The marriage took place just days after Oort's second husband died suddenly. For years there were rumors that either Kidd or Oort had somehow caused his death, but no evidence was ever found.

With property, a wife, and two stepdaughters, Kidd enjoyed the comfortable life of a family man and businessman in New York. He started a shipping company. He and his wife owned several houses, docks, and warehouses. Kidd dabbled in small-time privateering, attacking French boats around New York.

As Kidd mingled with the political leaders of the city and the colony, he met Robert Livingston, another man from Scotland who had come to New York. Livingston was ambitious and claimed to know people at King William's court. He convinced Kidd to sail to London in 1695. While there, Kidd would try to get a privateering license directly from the English government, which was looking for someone to hunt down troublesome pirates.

The Governor and the Pirates

From 1692 to 1697, England's colony of New York was overseen by Benjamin Fletcher, who had a reputation as a greedy and corrupt governor. While Fletcher was governor, pirates traveled openly in and out of New York Harbor. Pirate loot was sometimes stored in the city's warehouses and sold in its markets.

Fletcher was accused of giving letters of marque to captains with shady reputations. The letters of marque made it seem that captains were acting lawfully as privateers—but that wasn't always the case.

Thomas Tew, a privateer who turned pirate, was the cause of Fletcher's downfall. Tew received a letter of marque from Fletcher and in return promised him a share of whatever booty he got from raiding French ships. Many people believed that Fletcher knew all along that Tew planned on committing piracy, not privateering. Fletcher was accused of turning New York into a **haven** for villains such as Tew. In 1698, he was called back to England in disgrace.

three

The Last Voyage

Captain Kidd's last voyage made him famous—or notorious. It included piracy, treasure, murder, and **mutiny**, or rebellion by the crew. The voyage began in London in 1696. In a sense it ended there, too, with Kidd standing trial for his life.

The King's Pirate-Hunter

After Kidd arrived in London in 1695, he and Livingston met Richard Coote, the Earl of Bellomont. At the time, Bellomont was preparing to become the new governor of the New York and Massachusetts colonies,

Captain Kidd was believed to have buried a vast amount of treasure in the Caribbean.

Why a Galley?

Captain Kidd's privateering ship was dubbed *Adventure Galley* because it was a special kind of vessel: a **galley**. Used in the Mediterranean Sea since ancient times, a galley is a ship that has both sails and oars. When there is wind, a typical ship raises its sails and is pushed through the water by the force of the wind. What happens if the wind dies down, or if a ship has to enter waters that are sheltered from the wind? Without wind, a sailing vessel sits helpless on the sea.

A galley is different. If the wind fails, the crew sits on benches below the deck. With long oars on both sides of the ship, the men row as ordered by the captain above deck. Their manpower drives the ship forward. This means that a galley can move faster and

replacing Benjamin Fletcher. To prove to the people of New York that he was against piracy, unlike the man he was replacing, Bellomont urged King William to send a pirate-hunter after Tew and other pirates.

King William took Bellomont's advice. In addition to giving Kidd a letter of marque to capture French ships, he granted Kidd permission to arrest pirates wherever he found them. Kidd was allowed to keep any booty he captured, instead of having the courts decide who should get it.

A galley is a ship with both sails and oars.

steer more easily than a sailing ship when there is little or no wind.

A galley was a smart choice for pirate-hunting adventures. Pirates were often found in the shallow waters of bays, harbors, or channels between islands. Such places can be sheltered from the wind. In those conditions, a vessel with oars has the advantage. Kidd's *Adventure Galley* had another advantage, too: It was armed with thirty-four guns, or small cannons, to fire at French or pirate ships.

However, the king's permission included a strict warning: Kidd was forbidden to attack or bother any ships, people, or property that came from countries that were England's friends or allies.

Kidd, Bellomont, and Livingston made a deal to share the booty. Bellomont put up most of the money for Kidd's pirate-hunting ship, so he would get the largest share. In a separate deal, Bellomont promised to split his share of the booty with four powerful men who held high positions in the English government. A ten percent share of the booty was even supposed to go to King William.

Once Kidd was made the king's privateer and pirate-hunter, the partners raised money to build a new privateering vessel for Kidd. This ship, called the *Adventure Galley*, was built in Deptford, an area on the south bank of the River Thames in southeast London. In early 1696, Kidd was ready to assemble a crew for the *Adventure Galley*.

Crossing the Line

Historians do not agree on where Kidd found his privateering crew. Some say that he sailed to New York to say goodbye to his wife and signed on his crew there. Others say that he took on his crew in England, before sailing to New York. Either way, he picked about 150 men who signed on to be privateers. Kidd's crewmen would receive no pay, only a share of the booty. The crewmember who first sighted a prize—a ship for the *Adventure Galley* to attack—would win a cash bonus. Kidd's terms gave the crew a strong reason to go on the attack. If they returned from the voyage without taking any booty, the men would leave the ship empty-handed.

Unfortunately for Kidd, he soon lost more than half his crew. Soon after the *Adventure Galley* set sail, the ship was stopped by a ship of the Royal Navy, which had the right to take men it needed from any English vessel, whether the men wanted to "join" the navy or not. The Royal Navy ship's crew took some of Kidd's men to serve as sailors. This forced Kidd to return to port and replace the lost crewmen. He ended up with a less desirable bunch that included convicts and pirates. Then he set off for the Indian Ocean.

By April 1697, Kidd and the *Adventure Galley* were in the Indian Ocean, suffering from bad luck as the ship gradually fell into disrepair. He had not captured any pirates, and he had not attacked any French vessels. The ship was leaking. Some of the crew had already died of disease. Many of those who remained were restless and discontented. They talked of piracy. So far, the voyage was a failure.

A few months later the *Adventure Galley* attacked an Indiaman, a merchant ship belonging to England's East India Company. The Indiaman held off the attack, forcing Kidd to flee. The fact that Kidd would try attacking an English ship, however, suggests that he was crossing the line from privateer to pirate.

Soon after, the *Adventure Galley* captured a small trading vessel. The crew was from India, but the captain was English. Kidd's men boarded the trader, tortured some of the crew, and seized a small **hoard** of money. There was no reason to think that the trading vessel was French, which meant that Kidd had not acted as a privateer. By attacking the ship, he and his men had officially committed an act of piracy.

The Richest Prize

In the months that followed, the *Adventure Galley* cruised the Red Sea and the coast of India. Kidd's crew urged him to attack big merchant ships several times, but each time he refused. Kidd may have hoped to avoid being branded as a pirate, or he may have feared that an attack would fail.

Tension ran high between the captain and some of the crew. It rose to a tragic peak when crewman William Moore and Kidd got into an argument. Moore accused Kidd of ruining him because they had been at sea for some time but had gotten almost nothing for it. Kidd feared that such talk could lead to mutiny. To stop it, he angrily struck Moore in the head with a wooden bucket. The blow cracked Moore's skull, and he died of the injury.

Kidd had now committed a second serious crime. He may still have hoped that success as a privateer would keep him out of trouble—and finally success came his way. In late 1697, he used a trick to capture a French trading ship called the *Rouparelle*. As the *Adventure Galley* approached the *Rouparelle*, Kidd ordered his men to fly a flag that would identify the *Adventure Galley* as another French ship.

When Kidd boarded the *Rouparelle*, its captain presented him with a French **pass**—a document issued by the government of France registering the ship as one of its own. The *Rouparelle* was in fact a Dutch ship, not French, but many captains in those days carried passes and flags from more than one government, so that they could pretend to be on the same side as any privateer who tried to capture them. Kidd had tricked the captain of the *Rouparelle* into showing his French pass, which meant that Kidd could seize the *Rouparelle* and its cargo as a privateer, not a pirate.

Kidd sent some of his men aboard the *Rouparelle* to serve as its new officers. They followed the *Adventure Galley* to the coast of India, where

Kidd strikes crewmember William Moore with a fatal blow.

Kidd freed the crew of the *Rouparelle*. He sold its cargo of cloth to Indian traders, giving shares to his men, even though his contract with Bellomont and the other partners said that he was supposed to turn over all booty to Bellomont before it was divided into shares.

Kidd renamed the captured ship the *November*. Its new crew was made up of some of the men from the *Adventure Galley*. Kidd's luck seemed to have turned. He now had two ships, and after taking the *Rouparelle* he stopped and looted a few small foreign vessels. A few weeks later, in January of 1698, he took the biggest prize of his career.

The *Quedagh Merchant* was a large merchant vessel with an English captain. Its owners were from Armenia, an area of western Asia. A friend of the emperor of India had employed the Armenians and their ship. When Kidd approached the ship, he used the same trick that had worked on the *Rouparelle*—pretending to be French. When the captain of the *Quedagh Merchant* showed his own French pass, Kidd claimed the ship as a privateering prize. Was the *Quedagh Merchant* a lawful prize for an English privateer? England regarded the emperor of India as an ally, and Kidd had been forbidden to attack the friends and allies of England. True, the ship's captain had shown him a French pass—but Kidd himself had used such a pass. The *Quedagh Merchant* was no more a French ship than the *Adventure Galley* was.

Kidd, however, wanted to give up the prize ship. He may have feared that taking the *Quedagh Merchant* would cause trouble. Yet his crew insisted on keeping it, and Kidd gave in. The *Quedagh Merchant* was carrying a valuable cargo of goods such as cloth and iron. Once again, Kidd sold most of the cargo on the coast of India, receiving gold and silver in return. He assigned members of his crew to the newly captured ship.

Mutiny at Madagascar

Kidd's next move was to repair the *Adventure Galley*, which was leaking badly. He sailed to Madagascar, with the *November* and the *Quedagh Merchant* following him. Madagascar was a haunt of pirates, as Kidd the "pirate-hunter" knew. Whom did he meet there? Robert Culliford, the crewman-turned-pirate who had stolen Kidd's *Blessed William* years earlier in the Caribbean.

Instead of rushing to arrest Culliford, Kidd decided to repair his galley. Meanwhile, most of Kidd's men were in an uproar. Kidd had planned to return to America and meet with Bellomont to share out the booty from the *Quedagh Merchant*. The men, tired of sailing with Kidd, called for piracy instead and staged a mutiny against Kidd. Many joined Culliford's crew even after Kidd shared out the booty with them.

The *Adventure Galley* was too damaged to sail again. As for the *November*, the deserters from Kidd's crew stripped it of everything useful and burned what remained. Kidd was left with the *Quedagh Merchant* and fewer than twenty men from his original crew. He renamed his last ship

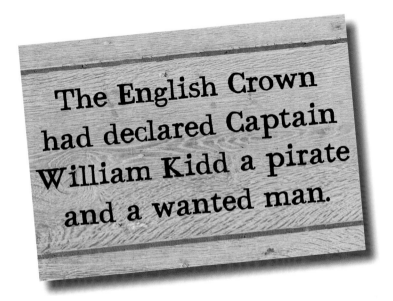

The English Crown had declared Captain William Kidd a pirate and a wanted man.

the *Adventure Prize* and convinced seafarers in Madagascar to join his crew. A few of them were well-known pirates. In November 1698, Kidd set out for home in the *Adventure Prize*. Five months later, he reached the Caribbean Island of Anguilla, where he stopped for water and supplies. There he received bad news: The English Crown had declared Captain William Kidd a pirate and a wanted man.

four

Death, Treasure, and Legends

Captain Kidd had set out on what was supposed to be a grand voyage of privateering and pirate-hunting, and returned to find himself a criminal. An English court would decide his fate. Centuries later, questions remain unanswered. Did he get a fair trial? Does his treasure still lie hidden somewhere, waiting to be found?

From Privateer to Prisoner

Once Kidd learned that he was considered a pirate, he wanted to rid himself of the *Adventure Prize*. Since the ship had been built in India for use in the merchant trade, it could be used as evidence—Kidd had

Kidd orders his men to hide his pirate loot.

captured it illegally. On the Caribbean island of Hispaniola—another pirate haunt—Kidd abandoned the *Adventure Prize* and purchased a smaller vessel called a **sloop**. He sailed to Boston, where Bellomont now lived as governor, with stops along the way in New Jersey and Long Island, close to New York City.

Kidd had hoped that Bellomont would pardon him after hearing his story. He believed that the French passes from the *Rouparelle* and the *Quedagh Merchant* would show that he was acting as a privateer, not a pirate. He gave the passes to Bellomont, his partner, for safekeeping. The governor's next move came as a shock to Kidd: Bellomont had Kidd arrested and sent to London to stand trial. No doubt Kidd felt betrayed by Bellomont, who gave the passes to his friends in the English government instead of returning them to Kidd. Historian and author Tim Travers, who has taught courses in the history of piracy, points out that Bellomont would not have wanted to be seen as a pirate-friendly governor, as Benjamin Fletcher had been.

Political forces were lined up against Kidd, too. The English Crown had declared Kidd a pirate because the emperor of India was furious over the loss of the *Quedagh Merchant*. Now the rich and powerful men in the English government who had backed Kidd's voyage wanted nothing to do with him. They did not stand up for Kidd. In fact, they made things worse for him. They conveniently "lost" the French passes that Kidd desperately needed to produce, as well as the agreements that identified those who

Kidd's corpse hangs as a warning to would-be pirates.

were supposed to profit from Kidd's voyage. (The lost passes turned up in 1910, when an American researcher discovered them in a London building used to store records from England's Board of Trade.)

Stories about Kidd's cruel and violent deeds began to spread, turning the public strongly against him. These stories may have been deliberately started by Kidd's former supporters as a **ploy** to ruin his reputation and get him out of the way. When Kidd went to trial in May 1701, he was found guilty of murdering William Moore and also of piracy against the *Rouparelle*, the *Quedagh Merchant*, and other ships. On May 23, 1701, Captain Kidd, after hearing his final sermon preached by Newgate Prison's chaplain, was hanged in London. His chained body was displayed at Tilbury Point, overlooking the River Thames. It hung there for a long time as a warning of the fate that awaited those seeking to commit piracy.

Captain Kidd at the Movies

The story of Captain Kidd has appeared on the movie screen more than once, although none of the movies has been close to **historical truth**. On screen, Kidd is portrayed as either "all hero" or "all villain."

The oldest known movie adaptation of Captain Kidd's life, entitled *Captain Kidd*, is a short film made in 1913. Nine years later, a serial version of the film told the story in fifteen episodes that were shown in theaters one at a time.

The early 1950s were a golden age of Captain Kidd movies, starting with *Double Crossbones* in 1951. In it, Captain Kidd is

Tales of Treasure

Although Kidd died, stories of his piratical adventures lived on—often ranging far from the truth. Some of the most long-lived tales involve a vast treasure of gold and jewels that Kidd was supposed to have buried or hidden somewhere before turning himself in to Bellomont.

Authors also have woven the legend of Kidd's lost treasure into exciting fiction. In 1834, American writer Edgar Allan Poe won the grand prize in a story contest for "The Gold-Bug," which is about a coded something of a "good guy." The following year the story took a humorous turn in *Abbott and Costello Meet Captain Kidd*. In it, comic actors Bud Abbott and Lou Costello played waiters who get hold of a treasure map. In *The Great Adventures of Captain Kidd* (1953), the captain is a heroic privateer in danger of being betrayed by his enemies. In *Captain Kidd and the Slave Girl* (1954), the captain falls in love with a woman who is put on his ship to spy on him.

One of the more popular movies is *Captain Kidd* (1945), starring Charles Laughton. Kidd is portrayed crudely as a bloodthirsty swashbuckler, but the overall quality of the film is high. The 1989 movie *George's Island* is about two children who try to find Kidd's treasure with the help of their eccentric grandfather. Kidd also appears in the 2006 television movie *Blackbeard*, which is mostly about Edward Teach, the pirate known as Blackbeard.

message that leads to Kidd's buried treasure on an island off the coast of South Carolina. The four books in Chris Archer's *Pyrates* series (2003) are about modern kids who are descendants of Captain Kidd and search for his treasure in caves beneath New York City.

Real-life treasure hunters have looked for Kidd's treasure, too. Kidd is known to have hidden several small chests of gold, silver, and other valuables on Gardiner's Island, near New York, which were recovered by Bellomont. Still, for several hundred years people have searched for more buried treasure on islands along the east coast of the United States and Canada. No more of Kidd's treasure, though, has ever been found.

Treasure hunters have also looked for Kidd's hoard in places he is not known to have visited, such as along the Hudson River in New York State. In 1983, a British and an American treasure hunter were arrested for trespassing in the Southeast Asian nation of Vietnam, where they were searching for Kidd's plunder.

Myth and Reality

Chests of glittering gold and jewels make for wonderful stories, but in reality there is no evidence that Kidd left a huge hoard of hidden treasure. While Kidd did acquire booty during his years as a privateer and pirate, most of it is accounted for. He took only one rich prize: the *Quedagh Merchant*. According to its owners, the value of its cargo was about equal to the money and goods that Kidd spent and Bellomont recovered.

Rumors of Kidd's great riches were probably just that—rumors. The *Quedagh Merchant*, though, is very real. In 2007, researchers from Indiana University uncovered cannons, anchors, and other wreckage from the ship in thirty feet of water off the coast of the Dominican Republic on the Caribbean island of Hispaniola, where Kidd abandoned the ship in 1699.

Other legends about Kidd fall short of the truth, too. He has sometimes been called a cruel, black-hearted villain. Other have called him an honorable privateer, who was betrayed by mutinous crewmen and selfish partners. The reality is most likely somewhere in the middle.

In 2007, archaeological divers from Indiana University recovered a cannon from Kidd's ship, the *Quedagh Merchant*. To preserve the cannon, it was stored in water.

Throughout his life, Captain Kidd demonstrated the qualities of both a ruthless pirate and the victim of circumstances beyond his control. He did not keep his men from torturing the crew of one of their prizes, even if he did not take part. He killed William Moore, although he probably did not intend to commit murder. Although Kidd did not receive a fair trial (because certain people in the English government wanted him out of the way so their ties to him would be hidden), he did commit the crimes for which he was convicted. Kidd lived in a time when people won fortunes at sea through both lawful privateering and unlawful piracy. Like many others, he found the line between the two easy to cross.

Timeline

1654   William Kidd is born in Dundee, Scotland

1689–1690 Kidd becomes a privateer for the governor of Nevis, an island in the Caribbean Sea

1691   Kidd settles in New York City and gets married

1692–1697 Benjamin Fletcher is governor of New York

1695   Kidd receives a letter of marque to become a privateer and pirate-hunter for the English Crown

1696   Kidd begins his privateering voyage in the *Adventure Galley*

1697   The *Adventure Galley* visits Madagascar; Kidd kills William Moore, one of his crew, with a bucket

1698   Kidd captures the *Quedagh Merchant*, with a valuable cargo

1699	Kidd tries to plead his innocence to Governor Bellomont but is arrested in New York
1700	Kidd is imprisoned in London
1701	Kidd stands trial for murder and piracy; he is convicted of murder and hanged
1724	*A General History of the Robberies and Murders of the Most Notorious Pyrates* is published
1983	Treasure-hunters are arrested while searching for Kidd's treasure in Vietnam
2007	A team of researchers from Indiana University locate the sunken wreck of the *Quedagh Merchant* in the Caribbean

Glossary

booty Money, goods, or other loot obtained by piracy.

colonies Territories outside a country's borders that are claimed, controlled, or settled by that country.

Crown A general term for a monarch or royal government, as in "the English Crown."

galley A type of ship that has both sails and oars, good for use in conditions of little or no wind.

Golden Age of Piracy The period from the 1680s to about 1730, when piracy flourished in the Indian Ocean.

haven A safe place.

historical truth Something believed to be fact, especially if there is good evidence in the form of documents and witnesses.

hoard Wealth or goods that are gathered and hidden.

Indiamen Large sailing ships used for carrying cargo in the Indian Ocean trade routes.

investors Those who puts money into a business venture in exchange for a share of the future profits.

letter of marque The document that makes a sea captain a privateer by giving permission to attack ships belonging to enemy nations; also called a commission or a license.

Liberi The name of the free, democratic pirates of Madagascar—who were probably fictional.

mutiny An act of rebellion by sailors or crewmen against their captain or other officers.

pass A document identifying a ship as being licensed or registered to a particular country.

piracy Unlawful attacks on, or robbery of, ships or property by sea captains and their crews.

pirate-hunter A ship captain with a special mission to find and arrest pirates.

ploy A clever trick or plan used to get someone to do something.

privateer A sea captain who has a letter of marque authorizing attacks on enemy shipping.

prizes Ships captured at sea.

sloop A sailing boat with one mast.

trading posts Places where goods are exchanged for other goods or for money.

Find Out More

Books

Gilkerson, William. *A Thousand Years of Pirates*. Plattsburgh, NY: Tundra Books, 2010.

Hamilton, Sue. *Captain Kidd*. Minneapolis, MN: Abdo Group, 2007.

Krull, Kathleen. *Lives of the Pirates*. New York, NY: HMH Books for Young Readers, 2010.

Websites

A Brief History of Piracy

www.royalnavalmuseum.org/info_sheets_piracy.htm

The Royal Naval Museum of Great Britain explains what piracy is, with a short overview of the history of pirates.

Captain Kidd (1645–1701)

www.portcities.org.uk/london/server/show/ConFactFile.3/Captain-Kidd.html

The Royal Museum at Greenwich, England hosts this site about the history of English seaports. There is a short biography of Captain Kidd, with links to other information about seafaring and piracy.

Captain Kidd: Pirate's Treasure Buried in the Connecticut River

www.bio.umass.edu/biology/conn.river/kidd.html

The University of Massachusetts' webpage about the legends of Captain Kidd's treasure, which some say was buried on an island in the Connecticut River.

Museums

The St. Augustine Pirate and Treasure Museum

www.thepiratemuseum.com

This interactive museum covers 300 years of pirate history, and boasts many artifacts including pirate loot, a real treasure chest, and one of only three surviving Jolly Roger flags.

The New England Pirate Museum

www.piratemuseum.com/pirate.html

Located in Salem, Massachusetts, this museum features a walking tour through the world of pirates, including recreations of a dockside village, ship, and a cave. Also on display are authentic pirate treasures.

The Pirates of Nassau

www.pirates-of-nassau.com/home.htm

Nassau was a pirate sanctuary for many years, welcoming Black Bart and many other noted pirates. This museum, located in the Bahamas, celebrates their exciting history.

The Queen Anne's Revenge Lab

www.qaronline.org

The researchers at the East Carolina University's West Research Campus in Greenville, North Carolina, have spent years collecting and analyzing artifacts from Blackbeard's famous flagship, *The Queen Anne's Revenge*, which sank just before Roberts was active. The artifacts are similar to items that would have been on Roberts' ships. The lab offers occasional tours, open houses, and traveling exhibits.

Bibliography

Clifford, Barry, with Paul Perry. *Return to Treasure Island and the Search for Captain Kidd.* New York, NY: HarperCollins, 2003.

Cordingly, David. *Under the Black Flag: The Romance and Reality of Life Among the Pirates.* New York, NY: Random House, 2013.

Howell, T.B., ed. "The Trial of Captain Wm. Kidd and others." *A Complete Collection of State Trials and Proceedings for High Treason and Other Crimes and Misdemeanors.* Vol. XIV. London, UK: T.C. Hansard, 1816. books.google.com/books?id=JENPSU6dlqoC&printsec=frontcover&source=gbs_ge_summary_r&cad=0#v=onepage&q&f=false

Konstam, Angus, with Roger Michael Kean. *Pirates: Predators of the Seas.* New York, NY: Skyhorse Publishing, 2007.

McFadden, David. "Captain Kidd's Ship Found Off Dominican Island." *National Geographic News.* Posted December 14, 2007. news.nationalgeographic.com/news/2007/12/071214-AP-caribbean-c.html

Ritchie, Robert C. *Captain Kidd and the War Against the Pirates.* Cambridge, MA: Harvard University Press, 1986.

Rogozinski, Jan. *Pirates!* New York, NY: Facts On File, 1995.

Travers, Tim. *Pirates: A History.* Stroud, UK: Tempus Publishing, 2007.

Zacks, Richard. *The Pirate Hunter: The True Story of Captain Kidd.* New York, NY: Hyperion, 2002.

Index

About the Author

Rebecca Stefoff has written books for young readers on many topics in history, science, exploration, and literature. She is the author of the six-volume series Is It Science? (Cavendish Square, 2014) and the four-volume series Animal Behavior Revealed (Cavendish Square, 2014). Although she has scuba-dived in sunken shipwrecks in the Atlantic Ocean and the Caribbean Sea, she has yet to see her first pirate ship. You can learn more about Stefoff and her books for young readers at www.rebeccastefoff.com.